Map from Cosmopolitan World Atlas
1993 by Rand McNally, R.L. 92-S-197

Carranza
Socoltenango
Comitán
Guadalupe
Trinitaria
Presa de la Angostura
Las Delicias
CHIAPAS
Jaltenango de la Paz
Paso Hondo
Chicomuselo
San Mateo Ixtatan
Barillas
Santa Eulalia
Concepción
Peten
MEXICO
GUATEMALA
MÉXICO
Chisec
PETÉN
San Luis
Poptún
TOLEDO
Monkey River
Casemero Palma
San Antonio
PUNTA NEGRA
14
RANGUANA CAY
Ranguana Entrance
NORTH SPOT
SAPODILLA CAYS
Gulf of Honduras
Port Honduras
Punta Gorda
PUNTA DE MANABIQUE
Bahía de Amatique
Livingston
Puerto Cortés
Bahía de Omoa
PUNTA SAL
Bahía de Tela
El Triunfo
Tela

El Pacayal
Jacaltenango
Motozintla de Mendoza
Concepción
HUEHUETENANGO
Amatenango de la Frontera
ALTA VERAPAZ
IZABAL
Cahabón
San Juan
Morales
Cobán
San Pedro Carchá
SIERRA DE SANTA CRUZ
CASTILLO DE SAN FELIPE
Lago de Izabal
El Estor
Izabal
MONTAÑAS DEL MICO
Puerto Barrios
Cuyamel
Choloma

Escuintla
2883
SIERRA MADRE
Concepción Tutuapa
Túxtla Chico
Tacaná
Volcán Tacaná 4093
Volcán Tajumulco 4220
SAN MARCOS
San Pedro
Sacatepéquez
Cuilco
QUICHÉ
CUCHUMATANES
Chajul
San Juan Cotzal
Nebaj
2739
3786
San Cristóbal Verapaz
BAJA VERAPAZ
Senahú
Panzós
Polochic
Cerro San Ildefonso 2228
Cofradía
Lima Nueva
Villanueva
HONDURAS
GUATEMALA
CORTÉS
Macuelizo
San Pedro Sula
Chamelecón
El Progreso
1067

Tapachula
Ciudad Hidalgo
Huixtlán
Huehuetán
Cacahoatán
Volcán Tacaná
San Marcos
Salcajá
Santa Cruz del Quiché
Chichicastenango
TOTONI-CAPÁN
Santa Cruz del Quiché
Zacualpa
3139
San Jerónimo
Salamá
Rabinal
SIERRA DE LAS MINAS
Los Amates
Gualán
ZACAPA
Zacapa
1716
QUIRIGUA
Azacualpa
San Marcos
Potrerillos
Cerro Cuchilla Alta 1737
Santa Rita
SANTA BÁRBARA
El Negrito
Morazán
Pico Pijol 2282
2744

San Marcos
San Pedro
Sacatepéquez
QUEZAL-TENANGO
Quezaltenango
3772
Almolonga
Volcán Santa María
TOTONICAPÁN
SOLOLÁ
Sololá
Patzún
CHIMAL TENANGO
Tecpán Guatemala
Comalapa
San Juan Sacatepéquez
Volcán Jumay 2176
EL PROGRESO
El Progreso
Jocotán
Chiquimula
CHIQUIMULA
COPÁN
Copán
Santa Rosa de Copán
Naranjito
Santa Bárbara
Arada
Las Vegas
Taulabé
La Libertad
COMAYAGUA

Ciudad Tecún Umán
Coatepeque
Retalhuleu
San Sebastián
Mazatenango
Suchitepéquez
3537
Santiago Atitlán
San Antonio Atitlán
Volcán Atitlán 3976
Ciudad Vieja
Antigua Guatemala
Volcán de Agua 3766
Palín
GUATEMALA
Guatemala
Amatitlán
Villa Nueva
San Pedro Pinula
JALAPA
Jalapa
San Luis Jilotepeque
Esquipulas
Quezaltepeque
2418
Corquín
Nueva Ocotepeque
OCOTEPEQUE
Gracias
Cerro Azul 2225
Cerro Las Minas 2849
CORDILLERA
INTIBUCÁ
Intibucá
La Esperanza
Jesús de Otoro
Siguatepeque
Comayagua
MONTAÑA
Ajuterique
La Paz
Villa de
San Antonio

Ocós
RETALHULEU
El Manchón
Champerico
Nueva Venecia
Santa Marta
Barrita Vieja
Puerto de San José
Buena Vista
Tiquisate
La Gomera
Santa Lucía Cotzalmaguapa
Masagua
ESCUINTLA
Escuintla
Palín
Barberena
Cuilapa
SANTA ROSA
Taxisco
Volcán Tecuamburro 1840
Chiquimulilla
Guazacapán
El Adelanto
JUTIAPA
Jutiapa
Volcán Moyuta 1662
Asunción Mita
Metapán
San Sebastián
La Palma
San Marcos
Concepción Quezaltepeque
Chalatenango
Aguilares
EL SALVADOR
Nueva Concepción
LEMPIRA
Sensuntepeque
Carolina
Ciudad Barrios
Corinto
San Francisco Gotera
Santa Rosa de Lima
LA PAZ
MONTAÑA LA SIERRA
Langue
Goascorán
VALLE
Nacaome
Sabanagrande

Garita Palmera
Acajutla
PUNTA REMEDIOS
Sonsonate
SONSONATE
Nueva San Salvador
San Salvador
Izalco
Nahuizalco
Volcán de San Salvador 1960
Mejicanos
Soyapango
Delgado
Apopa
Ilobasco
Cojutepeque
Guatajiagua
Jiquilisco
San Sebastián
Lolotique
Estanzuelas
Jocoro
Usulután
Jucuapa
Chinameca
San Rafael Oriente
El Transito
San Miguel
Volcán de San Miguel 2130
La Unión
Amapala
ISLA EL TIGRE
Golfo de Fonseca
Marcala

Santa Ana
Chalchuapa
Ahuachapán
Atiquizaya
Concepción de Ataco
Volcán de Santa Ana 2365
Lago de Coatepeque
Congo
San Vicente
Zacatecoluca
Volcán de San Vicente 2181
La Libertad
San Marcos
San Marcelino
La Tasajera
Jiquilisco
Chirilagua
El Cuco
Tamarindo
Volcán de Conchagua
Conchagua
PUNTA AMAPALA
PUNTA COSIGÜINA
Volcán Cosigüina 859
Estero
Puerto
Volcán
El China

▽ 5347
▽ 6349
▽ 5137
▽ 3737
▽ 3529
▽ 5356
▽ 5322
▽ 3387
▽ 2933
▽ 4014

PACIFIC

Enchantment of the World

GUATEMALA

By Marlene Targ Brill
and
Harry R. Targ

Consultant for Guatemala: George I. Blanksten, Ph.D., Professor Emeritus of Political Science, Northwestern University, Evanston, Illinois

Consultant for Reading: Robert L. Hillerich, Ph.D., Visiting Professor, University of South Florida; Consultant, Pinellas County Schools, Florida

CHILDRENS PRESS ®
CHICAGO

A flower seller in the market in Chichicastenango

Project Editor: Mary Reidy
Design: Margrit Fiddle

Library of Congress Cataloging-in-Publication Data

Brill, Marlene Targ.
  Guatemala / by Marlene Targ Brill and Harry R. Targ.
    p.   cm. — (Enchantment of the world)
  Includes index.
  Summary: Describes the geography, history, culture,
industry, and people of the Central American country
shaped by strong Spanish and Mayan influences.
  ISBN 0-516-02614-3
  1. Guatemala—Description and travel—1981—
Juvenile literature. 2. Guatemala—History—Juvenile
literature. [1. Guatemala.] I. Targ, Harry R.
II. Title. III. Series.
F1463.2.B74   1993   92-39099
972.81—dc20   CIP
                                            AC

Picture Acknowledgments
AP/Wide World Photos: 21, 51 (left), 53, 54, 55, 56, 57, 60,
61, 62 (2 photos)
© **John Elk III:** 16, 23, 68 (left), 71 (right), 76 (right), 77, 84,
88 (left), 90
© **Virginia R. Grimes:** 4, 33 (left)
H. Armstrong Roberts: © E. R. Degginger, 66 (left), 71
(left), 92 (bottom); © L. Jacobs, 67 (left); © C. Bryant, 82
Historical Pictures Service: 38, 47 (left)
© **Norma Morrison:** 67 (right)
North Wind Picture Archives: 44, 47 (right), 49

Odyssey/Frerck/Chicago: © Robert Frerck, 12 (left and
center), 32, 34 (left), 87 (right), 89 (right), 92 (top)
Chip and Rosa Maria de la Cueva Peterson: 5, 6
(bottom left), 10, 14, 15, 27 (right), 75, 88 (right), 104
(right)
Photri: 12 (right), 20 (left), 33 (right)
© **Carl Purcell:** 22 (right)
Root Resources: © Tom Brownold, 6 (top left), 19 (left),
76 (left), 78 (left); © Cory Langley, Cover, 13 (left); © Mary
A. Root, 19 (right), 24, 27 (left), 85 (left); © Kenneth W.
Fink, 28 (left); © Joyce Gregory Wyels, 68 (right); © Paul C.
Hodge, 91
Tom Stack & Associates: © Byron Augustin, 8; © Bob
Winsett, 86 (right)
Tony Stone Worldwide/Chicago: © Elizabeth Harris, 9,
13 (right), 78 (right), 104 (left); © Sarah Stone, 26;
© Robert Frerck, 34 (right), 74 (top), 87 (left); © Suzanne
Murphy, 70
SuperStock International, Inc.: 30; © N. Shah, 20 (right);
© K. Kummels, 48, 98, 99, 108; © M. Heitner, 25, 65; © G.
Martin, 51 (right), 80 (inset); © G. Riccato, 66 (right), 86
(left), 89 (left), 101; © M. Mattson, 74 (bottom);
© Lawrence Cherney, 80; © G. DeSteinheil, 85 (right), 94,
97; © D. Newman, 103 (right)
Valan: © Aubrey Lang, 6 (top right); © Stephen J.
Krasemann, 6 (bottom right); © Prof. R. C. Simpson, 28
(top center); © Sylvain Majeau, 28 (top right); © B. Lyon,
28 (bottom right); © Jean-Marie Jro, 103 (bottom left)
© **Karen Yops:** 16 (inset), 22 (left), 82 (inset), 103 (top left),
120
Len W. Meents: Maps on 82, 88, 93
**Courtesy Flag Research Center, Winchester,
Massachusetts 01890:** Flag on back cover
Cover: Market at Chichicastenango

Men of Nahualá still wear the traditional trajes, *a checked wool skirt, with a black wool jacket.*

TABLE OF CONTENTS

Colorful Guatemalan fabrics
rival the colors of nature.
Clockwise from left are:
a Nahualá baby wearing a
bright knitted hat,
Chichicastenango women in
the flower market, a scarlet
macaw, and a purple orchid

Chapter 1

A COUNTRY OF
MANY COLORS

Guatemala's story reveals a tale of conflict. The story tells how two cultures in one country clash. One Guatemalan culture includes the descendants of pre-Columbian Maya Indians. These people treasure their old ways. They live in villages known for multicolored costumes, crafts, and marketplaces.

Another main cultural group traveled from Spain to what became Guatemala more than four and one half centuries ago. Through the years, they tried to impose their Spanish ways of living on the people they called Indians. Spaniards brought their own colorful architecture, religion, and customs.

Guatemala became a country separate from Spain more than a century ago. Yet both cultures remain in conflict over this colorful land. The land occupies a region that contains landforms and plant life as varied as its people. There are many vivid shades of birds, flowers, and animals. There are crystal blue lakes, rich green shrubbery, black sand beaches, and active volcanoes with white smoke rising from the top.

Modern city buildings glisten in the ever-present sun, and historic ruins may be glimpsed through the overgrowth of brush.

Guatemala City

City workers shop in supermarkets and drive cars, while villagers sell handmade goods in local markets and work the soil with simple tools. These are the many colors of Guatemala. These are the shades that make this country one of the most fascinating yet most troubled in Latin America.

OLD AND NEW GUATEMALA

Few differences exist between Guatemalan and other Western cities worldwide. However, there are major contrasts between city and country life within Guatemalan borders.

In the larger cities live many Guatemalans who are descended from the Spanish colonists. These people work in high-rise office buildings. Their workweek typically runs Monday through Friday from 8:00 A.M. until 6:00 P.M. Businesses and schools close for lunch in the middle of the day.

Wealthy city folk travel by bus or taxi along wide boulevards and tree-lined residential streets. Children and adults wear

Left: A market woman sews while she waits for customers to buy her clothing and fabric.
Right: The jacket of this man from Solola has the raised pattern for which this region is known.

Both men and women still wear *tzutes*, Maya head cloths. When unwound, the cloths double as carrying sacks or baby slings. Many Maya continue to go barefoot like their ancestors. However, today families go without shoes mainly because they do not have the money to buy them. Some villagers make cheap sandals from old rubber tires.

In the warm and temperate regions, clothing is woven from cotton. Wool is used in the colder mountain regions. Delicate patterns woven into these garments indicate the wearer's social standing, marital status, group, or village. For example, the design of a Chichicastenango man's costume represents his marital status, the number of children he has, and how many of his sons are married. Solola men are known by the raised pattern on their jackets.

Hundreds of varied colors and designs are woven into the cloth, each with its own historical meaning. The Ixchel Museum in Guatemala City displays more than 5,000 examples of handmade costumes that represent 145 different Maya groups.

Markets provide opportunity to meet with people from other villages.
Indians recognize each other by their distinctive clothes (above and opposite page).

MARKETS

Nowhere are multicolored costumes displayed more vividly than at village and regional markets. Except in cities, most buying and selling occurs in these markets. Families sell their agricultural goods and crafts and buy basic needs here.

Merchants arrive by foot, mule, bus, or boat. Sometimes, they walk for hours to reach a bus route or market. Most often, the merchants are women. Women carry the goods for sale balanced on their heads in woven baskets or clay pots. Once at the market, they display the goods in baskets or on mats placed on the ground. The peddlers spend the day making or processing additional goods to sell. They weave baskets from leaves, clean vegetables, design cloth on hand looms, or sculpt wood carvings. Often, young children play nearby while their parents work.

Sellers and buyers decide on the prices by bargaining. A customer begins the process by asking the cost of an item. Whatever the answer, the customer offers to pay a lower price. The seller and the buyer go back and forth until they both agree

on a price. Often, it is only 75 percent of the original quoted price.

Bulk goods, like vegetables, are weighed on balance scales. A basket on one side of the scale holds a given amount. The merchandise to sell goes into a basket on the other side. The proper weight is determined when both baskets balance.

Regional markets draw people from many villages who want to sell their goods. Some come from twenty miles (thirty-two kilometers) away. Regional markets offer a broader variety of goods, including manufactured shoes, jeans, and candles. At these larger markets, villagers display their goods in open stalls.

Regional markets serve several functions besides selling goods. Markets located near churches present occasions for the people to pray to local saints. Additionally, markets provide isolated farmers with the opportunity to meet people from other villages. Indians recognize each other by their distinctive colorful clothing and lively crafts. They share news about conditions where they live and work, and they talk about their hope of selling enough that day to make a brighter tomorrow.

Guatemala's climate has no extremes, although the mountain valleys are chilly during the rainy season. Because of the mild climate, flowers bloom year-round and colorful birds make their home in the patio of this restaurant in Chichicastenango.

Chapter 2

LAND OF ETERNAL SPRING

Guatemalans, particularly in rural areas, have a special relationship with their land. Parents teach young children to respect the natural world. Youngsters learn that the earth feeds all humans and that life-giving water is sacred. The children discover that land is the main source of work for adults. Above all, the land has allowed their people and traditions to survive for centuries.

Guatemala is blessed with abundant natural resources. Its varied beauty is awesome. Deep canyons cut through high plains. Soaring mountains of rain forests surround mysterious caves and rumbling volcanoes. Few countries claim such a diversity of birds and animals combined with souvenirs of ancient civilizations.

The pleasant year-round climate gives Guatemala rich vegetation. In Guatemala City, the capital, colorful flowers are always blooming. The yellow palo blanco tree flowers in January, the bougainvillea in February, the purple nazareno in March, and on through the year. Guatemalans call their homeland "The Land of Eternal Spring."

BOUNDARIES

Guatemala covers about 42,042 square miles (108,889 square kilometers). The area is only slightly larger than the state of Ohio in the United States.

Four countries and two bodies of water share Guatemala's borders. Mexico, to the north and west, has the longest common boundary. Belize is on the east, and Honduras and El Salvador are to the southeast.

The Gulf of Honduras, an arm of the Caribbean Sea, stretches 53 miles (85 kilometers) along eastern Guatemala. The Caribbean coastline shelters the country's most important port of Puerto Barrios. The Pacific Ocean coastline extends 152 miles (245 kilometers) along southern Guatemala. Smaller Pacific ports that serve the area are San José and Champerico.

LAND AND ITS REGIONS—A WONDERLAND FROM NATURE

The many features of Guatemala can best be understood by dividing the country into four main regions: Pacific Coast, Highlands, Caribbean Coast, and Petén. Central mountain ranges crisscross southern Guatemala to create these divisions. The Sierra Madre parallels the Pacific Ocean. The Cuchumatanes Range runs from the middle of the country to the Caribbean. Formations branch off into other horizontal ridges that extend from Mexico to Costa Rica. Mountains and waterways in and around Guatemala contribute to the variety of landforms, climate, crops, and wildlife.

PACIFIC COAST

The Pacific Coast is mainly a flat treeless grassland. Its black sandy beaches sprinkled with palm trees extend from the Mexican border on the north to the southern border with El Salvador. A narrow plain averaging thirty miles (forty-eight kilometers) in width rises gently into the mountain Highlands.

18

A rain forest along the Polochic River (left) and
a black sand beach on the Pacific Coast

Scattered forests of rich jungle vegetation and broadleaved mangrove trees line the larger rivers that flow southward from the mountains. Eighteen rivers run to the Pacific Coast. However, many are short and difficult to navigate. Only three can be used for transportation by small boats. The longest river is the Suchiate. This river allows transport for only 38 miles (61 kilometers) of its 94 miles (151 kilometers). Rivers that reach the Pacific Ocean are the Samalá, Coyolate, and Michatoyo. One government goal is to transform the water flow of these and many other rivers that drain from the mountains into hydroelectric power.

Altitude plays an important role in regulating temperature and rainfall in Guatemala's various regions. Conditions along the coast are hot and humid. From sea level to 2,500 feet (762 meters), average daily temperatures are 90 degrees Fahrenheit (32 degrees Celsius). Monsoon winds blow heavy rain to the area. During the rainy season, high winds and driving rain often damage crops. At other times, rain is so sparse that irrigation is needed.

Farms in the Highlands; harvesting sugarcane near the Pacific Coast (right)

Few people live in the lowlands. But the rich volcanic soil offers some of Guatemala's best farmland. Since the 1940s the area has been developed into large plantations where cattle are raised and sugarcane and cotton are produced. Varied marine life dominates the Pacific waters, offering the opportunity for a major fishing industry.

HIGHLANDS

The Highlands comprise the east-west mountain chain that spans more than half of the country. The largest mountain range is the Sierra Madre, which runs along the Pacific border. Its highest peaks are to the west. Volcán Tajumulco, the largest, is the tallest mountain in Central America. It rises 13,845 feet (4,220 meters) above sea level.

The mountains hold much of Guatemala's natural splendor. Yet they provide cause for disaster as well. Guatemala has thirty-four

Workers cleaning up after the 1976 earthquake that killed approximately eighteen thousand people

volcanoes. Many Sierra Madre mountains are former volcanoes. A few are still active and could erupt at any time. Earthquakes are also a problem throughout the Highlands. In 1717 and 1773, earthquakes from Volcán Agua destroyed the second colonial capital city of Antigua. Santa María Volcán leveled the second-largest city, Quezaltenango, in 1902. And a series of earthquakes damaged Guatemala City early in the twentieth century. In 1976 the worst earthquake to date struck more than 8 percent of the nation. Some thirty thousand people died, and 20 percent of the people lost their homes.

Many Pacific Coast rivers originate in the Highlands. Similar to the coastal waters, Highland rivers tend to be short and navigable for short distances only. However, two large lakes surpass all others in size and beauty. Villagers and tourists alike claim that Lake Atitlán is the most beautiful lake in the world. Three volcanoes and many villages meet its shores. The lake has an area

of 176 square miles (456 square kilometers) and is 990 feet (302 meters) deep in some places. More recently, some owners of vacation homes and hotels have dumped sewage into lake water shared by the Maya, who use the water for washing clothes, fishing, and bathing.

Lake Amatitlán is smaller and less scenic than Lake Atitlán. Still, this lake is unique for its warm steamy water and medicinal sulfur springs. The water gets these qualities from the nearby Volcán de Pacaya, an active volano that last erupted in 1964.

Mountain regions have more definite seasons than the coast. The mild temperatures range from 60 degrees to 70 degrees Fahrenheit (16 degrees to 21 degrees Celsius) throughout most of the area. However, at elevations above 5,500 feet (1,676 meters), temperatures can drop quickly. Mountain nights can be chilly,

Highland village of San Mateo Ixtatán

especially during the rainy season. The rainy season lasts from
May until November, when rain falls almost daily.

Beautiful mountains, trees, lakes, fertile volcanic soil, and
abundant rainfall for growing crops make the mountains a
desirable place to live and work. Consequently, most Guatemalans
live in the Highlands. Guatemala City, the nation's largest city,
lies on a Highland plateau. Indians farm small plots of corn and
beans on mountain slopes in the west, where temperatures are
most temperate. The warmer, wetter northern region produces
most of the country's coffee.

Steep, rugged mountains and jagged waterways have divided
the country into isolated pockets for centuries. Independent
villages were able to maintain their own languages and customs
because the land restricted contact with both other rural people
and people from the more modern cities.

The Motagua River

CARIBBEAN COAST

The Caribbean Coast is Guatemala's lowland region to the east. Here unspoiled beaches meet the Caribbean Sea at the Gulf of Honduras. The region is noted for having the country's largest lake, Lago de Izabal, which has an area of 228 square miles (591 square kilometers).

The Caribbean region has three main river valleys that are separated by mountains. These valleys link the coast to other parts of Guatemala. The Motagua, Guatemala's longest river, rises in the Highlands and flows for 250 miles (402 kilometers). One hundred of these miles are navigable. Railroads and highways follow the river from Guatemala City to the coast. The Motagua Valley shapes the boundary between Guatemala and Honduras as the river empties into the Caribbean. Similarly, the Sarstún creates a natural border between Guatemala and its northeast neighbor,

Typical riverboats

Belize. The Dulce is the shortest and, perhaps, the most beautiful. Riverboats navigate its entire 24 miles (39 kilometers) through a valley surrounded by dense jungle.

Normally, storms rage over the Caribbean Sea. But the Bay of Amatique shelters 25 miles (40 kilometers) of Guatemala's eastern coastline from driving rains. Still, the climate is tropical and humid without relief. In this wettest part of Guatemala, rainfall can be as much as 200 inches (508 centimeters) a year. Tropical rain forests of evergreen mangrove trees thrive in the steamy heat. So do many crops important to Guatemala's economy. The eastern Motagua River Valley and the area around Lago de Izabal are centers for large banana plantations and production of fruits and vegetables that are shipped from the area's ports. Cargo ships to and from other Central American countries and the United States travel from Puerto Barrios and the smaller ports of Santo Tomás de Castilla and Livingston.

Jungle surrounds the ruins of the ancient Maya city of Tikal.

PETÉN

Petén covers about one-third of Guatemala's vast northern territory. Its land is a limestone plateau covered with jungles and occasional tropical grasslands. Many lakes and ponds are in this region, and rainfall can be very heavy. However the soil quickly drains into underground caves, leaving the earth too dry for planting crops. Consequently, few people live here, although ancient Maya civilization centered here sixteen hundred years ago. Cedar, mahogany, and other hardwood lumbering; the production of sapodilla, which produces chicle for gum; and rubber production dominate the region. Local residents harvest two popular Guatemalan fruits, the sapote from the chicle tree and the chicozapote.

Sunset at Lake Petén Itzá and a house in Petén's capital, Flores (inset)

The region's magic lies in the many Maya ruins throughout the area. Visitors especially treasure the limestone caves with pictures and hieroglyphic writing that were sites of religious ceremonies. These caves contain unusual rock formations. Spectacular stalagmites, rock formations projecting upward from the cave floor, and stalactites, cone-shaped mineral formations jutting down from a cave roof, reflect a frosty light.

Most people in the Petén region live around Lake Petén Itzá. Petén's capital, Flores, developed on a cone-shaped island connected to the lake's shore. Indian legend states that the lake will rise every fifty years. Indeed, rains overflowed the lake's banks in the early 1930s and early 1980s.

Native to Guatemala are the scarlet macaw (left), white orchids (top center), spider monkeys (bottom center), and toucans (top right).

PLANTS AND ANIMALS

Guatemala's diverse climates and landforms harbor more types of plants and animals than are found anywhere in the world. Wildlife experts count more than 885 kinds of mammals, birds, amphibians, and reptiles in the Sierra de las Minas mountains alone. There are common robins or wrens, the rare poc, which lives on the waters of Lake Atitlán, and colorful macaws or toucans.

Guatemala has eight thousand different types of plants, including six hundred species of orchids. The white nun orchid is the national flower. Orchids grow throughout Guatemala. Most Indians do not believe in picking flowers. They are to be shared by the community. However, white orchids are part of certain religious celebrations, such as weddings and funerals.

PRESERVING THE ENVIRONMENT

Such large numbers of natural resources mask a growing problem. As in other countries, modern life-styles threaten Guatemala's natural resources. Local, Central American, and worldwide groups have organized to preserve Guatemalan wildlife. The Guatemalan government created a network of national parks and recreation areas to offer environmental education and control habitats for endangered wildlife. Undeveloped land has been set aside or restricted against any development that would harm the environment.

One highland area is devoted to the quetzal, Guatemala's national bird. The quetzal has long flowing tail feathers of brilliant colors. Interest in the quetzal goes back to pre-Columbian times. The Maya believed the bird was a symbol of life. Priests and nobles wore long feathers as a sign of special power. Modern Guatemalans named their currency after this rare bird.

Other national parks protect forest and coastal vegetation that provides food and homes for wildlife. Most Guatemalans agree that future generations should enjoy the same natural resources that have existed since ancient times.

No one knows why the Maya built on such a grand scale at Tikal in the lowlands of the Petén. Without using wheels or iron tools, humans cut and carved stone to build these huge structures.

Chapter 3

PRIESTS, PYRAMIDS, AND KINGS

During the 1500s, Quiché scribes recorded their sacred history in *Popul Vuh, the Quiché Book of Counsel*, referred to as the "Bible of the Americas." This important book described the beginning of Maya civilization.

Ancient Maya wrote that the world began when their god, Tojil, struck his leather sandal with a stone. Suddenly, a spark flashed and continued to burn. The first light illuminated a calm sea and cloudless sky. Then the Heart of the Sky, the sun, ordered the earth to appear. Mountains were raised from the sea. Trees were rooted into the new earth.

Yellow and white ears of *maize*, or corn, grew from the divided waters. The Heart of the Sky made the first humans from this blessed corn. They were called Jaguar Quiché, Jaguar Night, Nought, and Wind Jaguar. These people gave rise to one of the most developed early civilizations in the Americas—the Maya.

In the past European scholars countered this legend by claiming that the early Maya originated from Aztec tribes of northern Mexico or the Inca of Peru and Ecuador. However, recent research from ancient ruins at El Mirador and Nakbe in Petén reveals that Maya civilization prospered before these other tribes appeared. Exact Maya origins are undecided as yet.

The Temple of the Giant Jaguar, built around A.D. 700, is 145 feet (44 meters) high.

Maya centers sprang up about A.D. 100. Newer tribes arrived to challenge the dominance of older tribes. Maya culture developed and expanded with each new tribe, reaching great heights between A.D. 250 and A.D. 900. Some historians call this the Classic Period or Golden Age.

During this time, the Maya built some two hundred cities in areas of what is now Mexico, Guatemala, Belize, and parts of El Salvador and Honduras. Maya civilization centered in the Petén jungle of northern Guatemala. The city of Tikal was one of the largest and oldest cities. Today, Tikal ruins reveal pyramids, palaces, temples, markets, and shrines—all reflecting the great Maya past.

CLASSIC MAYA ACHIEVEMENTS

The classic Maya distinguished themselves in art, science, and architecture. They transformed simple forms of writing and

Hieroglyphs (left) on a limestone stela
and a circular Maya calendar stone (right)

mathematics into complicated tools for communication and measurement. The Maya recorded their history in *hieroglyphs,* an involved picture language. Hieroglyphs have been found on limestone *stelae,* or tall writing slabs, flattened bark from fig trees, pottery, animal skins, and monument walls. Over the years, archaeologists have learned to decipher these signs. They discovered stories about battles, births, marriages, deaths, and new leadership.

The Maya created an accurate yearly calendar of 360 days, with 18 months of 20 days each and 5 extra days. The calendar allowed the Maya to count thousands of years into the past or future. However, leftover days were considered unlucky. On these days, people fasted and participated in ceremonies designed to prevent disaster. Afterward, they celebrated New Year's Day. A few Maya villages follow their ancestors' calendar to this day. The Maya invented the concept of zero at a time when most civilizations had no way to express the idea. They also advanced astronomy

Stelae are found at Quirigua, south of Lago de Izabal (left), as well as "Zoomorphs" (above), carved stones depicting mythical animals created by the Maya.

without the benefit of telescopes. These early scientists traced paths of planets and predicted solar and lunar eclipses.

Equally amazing, the Maya built pyramids, temples, and aqueducts without metal tools, wheels, and pack animals to cart materials.

CLASSIC MAYA SOCIETY

Classic Maya society had definite social groups or classes. Citizens were peasants, artisans, merchants, warriors, or priests. Another group was slaves who were captured in battle. Unlike slavery in North America, Maya slaves could buy their freedom and own property.

Early Maya communities were controlled by priests. Each village or city-state had its own religious leader. Village priests operated independently of leaders from other villages, although a network of priests kept in close contact.

After the Quiché were defeated, Spanish soldiers demanded soldiers, taxes, and women from the Cakchiquel. The Cakchiquel turned against their former allies. For the next ten years, the Cakchiquel battled the Spanish until they, too, were defeated. Some Maya were able to escape into isolated mountains. These groups continued to revolt against Spanish rule for the next two hundred years.

Between 70 and 90 percent of the Maya died from war or illness during the sixteenth century. Throughout Central America people died from the diseases brought by the Spanish. The Maya had few defenses against smallpox, influenza, and bubonic plague, to which they had never been exposed. Within one hundred years of the Spaniards' arrival, the Indians throughout Central America were almost totally wiped out.

The Indians who survived were enslaved or forced to work on land taken by the Spanish. The Spanish government sent Christian missionaries to reduce Maya resistance by converting them to Catholicism. The church burned most Maya writings and forced the Indians to honor Catholic saints and observe Catholic rituals. Conquering soldiers thought the priests were wasting their time on Indians whom they considered not even human. However, some missionaries opposed any violence and argued that the population was capable of being converted.

Guatemalan Maya gave Spain the most resistance in Central America. Survivors vigorously protected their culture. On the surface, they pretended to pray to the Christian God. Privately, the Maya were faithful to their own gods. Many Guatemalan communities still practice ancient ceremonies despite centuries of Spanish domination. Yet in most other Central American countries traditional cultures have been nearly destroyed.

SPANISH COLONIAL GOVERNMENT

At first, Spain established several administrative offices within the Maya empire. These offices operated independently and sometimes competed with each other. Then Spain created one government to bring greater order to cities and villages.

The first capital of Guatemala under Spanish control, founded in 1524, was called Santiago do los Caballeros. By the 1570s, Spain organized the Captaincy General of Guatemala to govern the area that is now Costa Rica, Nicaragua, Honduras, El Salvador, Guatemala, and southern Mexico. The seat of the Kingdom of Guatemala was in Antigua. An earthquake leveled Antigua in 1773 and the central government moved to Guatemala City. Representatives of the Spanish crown ruled from capital cities in each region. Mayors and local councils replaced tribal rule in villages.

COLONIAL ECONOMY

From the beginning conflicts arose over who controlled the new colony's economy. Spanish planters and merchants settling in Central America objected to Spain's trade regulations. *Criollos*, settlers of Spanish blood, opposed government control from the capital city. The Catholic church acquired vast tracts of land for their churches, convents, and monasteries, so the clergy wanted a voice in government, too. Indians struggled to survive in an economy forced on them. However, Indian interests were never seriously considered.

From the beginning, rigid separation of the classes was a way of life. Colonial government representatives were at the top of the social ladder with the wealthiest colonists. They claimed profits from Maya land on behalf of large trading companies in Spain. The next group were the criollos. They owned land and controlled most of the wealth not sent to Spain. Some criollos became wealthy merchants, monitoring the flow of goods from the countryside to Spain.

Priests gained considerable wealth in Guatemala. A Catholic church was built in every town. Spain granted the clergy large sections of land in the name of the church. The land generated many products for their use or trade. Priests organized and regulated education, mainly for Spaniards and to train more priests. They built Central America's first university in 1532. Within a short time the church claimed the souls, minds, and money of many Guatemalans.

A new class of people called ladinos arose. These people sought to better their economic life by separating themselves from the Maya culture and community. Like the Spanish, ladinos looked down on the Indians. But ladinos were never fully accepted among the criollo population or allowed to rise to wealthier classes guarded by Spaniards. Some ladinos worked for pay on rural plantations. Others struggled to survive in colonial cities. A few became artists, shopkeepers, or manufacturers.

The weakest and most mistreated people were the Indians. They were more likely to be poor and powerless. They experienced slavery, forced labor, and heavy taxation throughout the colonial period. To justify extreme differences in wealth, Spaniards claimed to be racially superior to the Indians.

Spaniards originally came to the Americas in search of riches, particularly gold and silver. After the Spanish conquest, Indians were forced to dig mines looking for gold. Within a short time,

Spain exhausted the limited resources. Then colonists turned to agriculture to produce goods for Spain to sell to other European traders.

Spanish and criollo planters needed plenty of land and a large work force to grow enough crops. The Spanish government established the New Laws of 1541 to force Indians into working for Spanish and criollo planters. *Encomienda* granted a small number of planters the right to seize Maya land and tax the Indians who lived there. The Indians who were unable to pay were expected to work land owned by whomever issued the decree. With *repartimiento,* another law for dividing the land, Indians were required to work for landowners who merely petitioned authorities for their services.

To keep Indians from escaping into the mountains, the colonial government adopted *reducción.* With this policy, the government moved thousands of Indians into seven hundred towns that were more centrally located. Here the government was able to control Maya revolts and convert the Indians to Christianity more easily. Reducción relocated the Maya closer to where labor was needed. More important, the policy freed land for Spanish planters to occupy.

Some planters moved from cities onto their large tracts of lands beyond city government control. They built large houses, or *haciendas,* that resembled homes in Spain. Haciendas had thick stucco walls and rooms encircling interior flowered patios.

The Spaniards introduced many firsts to the Central American economy. Horses and donkeys revolutionized transportation. Donkeys were used as pack animals and horses were used to ride and pull two-wheeled carts, the first vehicles with wheels in the region. Tamed livestock provided new products. Cattle were processed into leather, soap, candles, and food products. Hogs provided pork and lard, a fat for frying.

During the seventeenth century, cacao was the main export crop. The Spaniards also found they could profit growing sugarcane, corn, cotton, and tobacco and raising cattle. As the textile industry grew, demand for dyes emerged. Central America became a major producer of indigo, a blue-tinted dye.

DESTRUCTION OF THE SPANISH EMPIRE

By the late eighteenth century, Spain encountered problems holding onto its Central American colonies. Spain was at war with France and England, which strained the Spanish military.

England established a colony in Central America and began producing indigo. English colonies soon produced large amounts of indigo and sold it on the world market. These sales severely cut the demand for Guatemalan indigo.

Furthermore, criollos and ladinos objected to Spanish colonial policies that taxed merchants heavily and restricted their trade with other countries. Some Indian groups organized revolts to break free of Spanish abuses. All these forces called for change at a time when the North American colonies were fighting for their freedom.

First, Mexico announced its independence. Then a group of Central Americans in Guatemala City declared independence on September 15, 1821. By then, the Spanish colonial empire was too weak to resist the independence movement. Central Americans began the long process of establishing new political and economic systems to replace Spanish rule. After three hundred years, the Spanish colonial government of Central America ended.

Agustín de Iturbide

Chapter 5

EMERGENCE OF MODERN GUATEMALA

INDEPENDENCE

Independence triggered more than a century of conflict and harsh rule. At first, Mexican Emperor Agustín de Iturbide announced that Central America should unite under Mexico. Iturbide ordered soldiers throughout the region to guarantee his claim. Still, he never gained the foothold he needed.

Within two years, Mexicans overthrew Iturbide. On July 1, 1823, the provinces of Guatemala, Costa Rica, El Salvador, Honduras, and Nicaragua declared their independence from Mexico and formed their own loosely organized federation — the Central American Federation or United Provinces of Central America. Chiapas was the only province to remain part of Mexico.

THE UNITED FEDERATION

The federation's constitution created a united congress and senate but allowed provinces their own local government. Each province had a chief, vice chief, and supreme court. The capital of the federation was in Guatemala City. Additionally, the constitution made Catholicism the official religion, established voting rights, and abolished slavery for the first time in the Americas. Sadly, civil rights provisions were mainly for those who owned land. Life for the Indians barely changed.

Provincial leaders disagreed almost from the beginning. Two major clashing groups were the Conservatives and Liberals. Conservatives wanted to maintain a confederation with trade ties to Spain, the old colonial power. They determined that the Catholic church should retain control of education, marriages, and divorces. They believed the church should keep large sections of land, slaves, and cheap Indian labor. Basically, Conservatives preferred to keep Guatemala the way it was before Spanish colonization ended.

Liberals, including some large landowners from outside Guatemala City and smaller criollo and ladino landowners, favored trade with many countries free from ties to Spain. They tried to limit the church's political power and land holdings. They also sought to abolish slavery and create laws that gave limited equality to the Indians.

Debate between these groups continued for many years beyond the federation. Their ideas and their battles influenced much of Guatemalan politics. However, Liberal and Conservative debates were between two landowning groups. Neither had a vision of power that included those who owned little or nothing.

Before the federation collapsed in the 1830s, Liberal Mariano Gálvez became provincial leader of Guatemala. Gálvez reformed the government and reduced church power, making marriage, divorce, and education civil matters.

To stimulate economic growth, Gálvez favored manufacturing and production of coffee, sugar, and cochineal, a dye that had replaced indigo in importance. He proclaimed laws that opened Guatemala to foreign investment, which increased export and import trade. Britain quickly gained control of Guatemalan shipping interests. By 1839, 90 percent of Guatemala's imports were British products. Guatemala under Gálvez had traded the Spanish economic power for the British.

Increased exports required more crops. Liberals passed laws that secured land to grow these crops. The government seized estates owned by the church and land owned jointly by members of Indian communities. The loss of land renewed calls for revolt among Indians and poor ladinos.

PEASANT REVOLT

A one-time poor ladino named Rafael Carrera led the revolutionary movement that spread across Guatemala. Carrera heightened the protest after his wife was attacked and his property was burned. In 1839 he led an army to capture Guatemala City. Carrera established an independent government that replaced the United Provinces after the Central American Federation collapsed. He remained as Guatemala's leader until his death in 1865.

Carrera worked closely with landowners and merchants who opposed the Liberal policies of the past. He restored church control over education, marriage, and large tracts of land. He gave merchants authority to manage commerce and banking. Merchants who earlier had traded with Spain renewed agreements. Now the merchant class collected state revenues,

Left: Rafael Carrera encouraged the production of cotton and coffee. Right: Berries are picked by hand when they turn red. Inside each berry are two coffee beans.

constructed roads and harbors, and encouraged production of new crops, such as coffee and cotton.

Although Carrera favored landowners, merchants, and clergy, he provided some protection for poor Indians and ladinos. Indian culture was protected. Peasants retained their land. One historian claimed that Carrera was the only leader who gave Indians and poor ladinos a voice in national politics.

COFFEE AND BANANAS

When Carrera died in 1865, international trade was changing. Demand for cochineal and indigo declined as European textile manufacturers invented new chemical dyes. Guatemala's merchants and landowners searched for new products to sell worldwide.

The answer to this problem came with the growing demand for coffee. Beginning in the 1840s, Guatemala gradually shifted its

Justo Rufino Barrios decreed a vagrancy law that required anyone caught without a job to work on coffee plantations to increase production.

one-crop export economy from dyes to coffee. For a time Carrera's Conservative successors resisted efforts by coffee growers to expand land holdings to grow more. Carrera followers opposed attempts by Liberals to end Indian control over their communal land and villages. Liberals wanted all restrictions on Indian land ended. Once protections were lifted, Liberals could demand cheap labor from landless Indians.

Military officers responded to landowner protests. The army overthrew the Conservative administration. The 1871 revolution brought Liberal Justo Rufino Barrios to power. His government supported landowners and foreign investors in their desire to make coffee production the key to the Guatemalan economy. Under his direction, the government seized all shared land. Barrios reduced church power by taking church property and selling it.

Once growers had land, Barrios established the first of many rounds of vagrancy laws. These laws required anyone caught

A drawing of laborers going to work in the coffee plantations

without a job to work on plantations as punishment. Other laws authorized local officials to determine the number of villagers who would labor on large plantations and the time limits on their service.

In some instances, local agents traveled to Indian villages to offer advance wages as loans. These loans were to be repaid by providing labor. Loan agreements were then sold to large landowners. With this plan, the Indians eventually became indebted to landowners for service.

These policies made land and cheap labor available for increasing coffee production. The Guatemalan economy became attractive to foreign investors again. Funds poured in from Britain and Germany. Many Germans bought former church lands in Guatemala to grow coffee. They moved to Guatemala and intermarried. By the twentieth century, British and German businesspeople controlled a sizable portion of Guatemala's coffee production.

Although a harsh leader, Barrios carried out many political reforms. His government instituted the first popular election for president and the country's third constitution, which lasted another sixty-six years. He limited church power by declaring several laws to restrict Catholic activities. Many priests were expelled from the country, and others were silenced.

Barrios bolstered the economy by beginning to build roads and railroads. He brought electricity to Guatemala City and installed telegraph and telephone lines. Barrios expanded the national banking system that had begun in 1731.

In education Barrios sought to have free, compulsory schools for all children between the ages of six and fourteen. However, he died in 1885 without fulfilling this dream. At the time Barrios was in El Salvador following another dream. Barrios was killed forming an army to reestablish another Central American federation.

Liberal governments after Barrios changed the future of Guatemala by establishing economic ties with the United States. The most striking example was an arrangement with Minor Cooper Keith, a developer from Boston. At the time, Keith headed the International Railways of Central America (IRCA). He wanted to expand tracks through Costa Rica and Guatemala. Keith's excuse was the demand for shipment of products. During the 1890s, Keith began growing bananas in both countries to justify expansion of his railroad and shipping facilities.

Bananas became such a profitable crop that Keith formed the Boston-based United Fruit Company and became its vice-president. The United Fruit Company worked closely with the IRCA and United Fruit Steamship Company. Over the next thirty years, these companies acquired large amounts of Guatemalan

Workers are clearing land to prepare to plant banana palms (left). Bananas for sale in a market (right)

land. Their resources dominated Guatemala's transportation and public services industries. The United Fruit Company soon influenced political and economic life throughout Central America.

WORLD WARS AFFECT GUATEMALAN BUSINESS

German investments declined during World War I, and after the war they practically stopped. Germany had enough to do with rebuilding its own economy. By the 1920s United States investors, particularly from the United Fruit Company, had replaced the Germans. Now United States business interests dictated Guatemalan politics, as Spain, England, and Germany had done earlier.

The shift in crops and investors brought little change for the Indians. They were still kept from education, power, and wealth. One major reason was that few of the Indians learned Spanish, the national language. Most retained the languages of their ancestors. To learn Spanish was like becoming a ladino. Those who learned ladino language and customs were rejected by the community. Even Indians who worshiped Christian saints and holidays did so only as they coincided with gods of nature and planting cycles. Secretly, most Indians remained true to Maya traditions.

The Liberals claimed that the Indians stayed poor because they were inferior as a group. Therefore, they were incapable of improving their lot. Lawmakers used this false reasoning to force labor, steal communal land, and deprive Indians of economic independence.

Some ladinos advanced as merchants or took advantage of industrial expansion in cities. Others joined the growing military. These ladinos gained more acceptance in politics and the economy. However, poor ladinos were no better off than the Indians. Many flocked into overcrowded cities in search of the few manufacturing jobs. Factories and cities were unprepared to absorb large numbers of poor people, especially those who knew little Spanish and had few skills beyond simple farming and crafts.

Problems of poverty, unemployment, and inequality increased during the late 1920s when the worldwide Great Depression started. The poor economy led to renewed conflicts in Guatemala.

One military leader who tried to bring order to the unsteady nation by crushing any opposition was General Jorge Ubico. He was elected president in 1930. Military force helped him stay in power for fourteen years. Soldiers killed or jailed any students, labor organizers, soldiers, or politicians who opposed their president.

Ubico enacted new vagrancy laws that required Indians to carry

General Jorge Ubico was president of Guatemala from 1930 to 1944.

a passbook. The passbook had to show that the person carrying it worked at least 150 days a year. The only way for landless people and small landowners to provide proof was to work for wealthy landholders.

Ubico created other regulations that favored large landowners and foreign businesses. When the demand for Guatemalan products in other countries was low, Ubico offered loans and granted tax relief to large landowners and businesspeople. The United Fruit Company continued to earn high profits without paying local property taxes or import duties on raw materials. The company's empire now included a port, shipping line, and radio and telegraph company in Guatemala.

Ubico supported the United States entry into World War II against his old ally, Germany. He allowed the United States to station troops in Guatemala and bought United States war bonds.

Juan José Arévalo was elected president in 1944. He introduced labor and economic reforms.

He also seized German property and permitted the United States to move Germans who were Guatemalan citizens into internment camps in Texas.

In 1944 some Guatemalan soldiers, students, and middle-class professionals forced Ubico from office. Later that year an election brought Juan José Arévalo, a university professor, to the presidency.

BEGINNING OF REFORM

Arévalo introduced many economic reforms. He abolished the vagrancy laws that supported forced labor. He raised the minimum wage and he allowed peasants to organize unions to represent their interests.

A new labor code required corporations to negotiate disputes with workers. It called for restricted work hours for women and

Colonel Jacobo Arbenz Guzmán delivering his inaugural address in 1951

children, better working conditions, and the right to strike. Now workers and peasants had a small but definite voice in Guatemalan politics. After 125 years of repression, poor Guatemalans—both Indians and ladinos—had some hope.

Colonel Jacobo Arbenz Guzmán, a landowner and military officer, became president after the 1950 elections. Arbenz expanded reforms started by Arévalo. He raised minimum wages to more than one dollar a day. For a while, general living standards improved slightly for factory workers and farm laborers. With another bold move, Arbenz forced landowners to pay taxes on their profits.

However, Arbenz's most significant actions were in land reform. His reform program required the government to take control of any unused agricultural lands or land acquired illegally. This land was to be redistributed to Indians and poor ladinos for farming. Large landowners opposed losing land, even if they

United States President Dwight Eisenhower (left) and
his Secretary of State John Foster Dulles said that the
Communists were ruling Guatemala.

received payment in exchange. They argued that the payment was
too little and too late.

The angriest landowner was the United Fruit Company. By
then, the United States company owned huge tracts of land
throughout Guatemala, including a large percentage that
remained unplanted. United Fruit's practice was to allow land to
lie fallow from time to time. The revolutionary government
regarded this land as unused and belonging to Guatemala. In one
province alone, United Fruit lost 234,474 acres (95,000 hectares) of
land.

United Fruit complained to the United States government. The
administration of President Dwight Eisenhower sympathized with
the company. Several men from Eisenhower's administration
either worked for or had interests in United Fruit. At their urging,
Eisenhower organized a small military force of anti-Arbenz
Guatemalans who had sought exile in Honduras and other
neighboring countries. He and Secretary of State John Foster Dulles
charged that Guatemala was ruled by friends of the Soviet Union,
then a Communist state and potential enemy of the United States.

President Carlos Castillo Armas reversed the reforms started with President Arévalo.

About two hundred troops and six planes invaded Guatemala from Honduras on June 18, 1954. The United States air force backed the group by threatening to bomb Guatemala City if the Guatemalan military continued to support Arbenz. He was forced to flee. United States Ambassador John Puerifoy chose the new head of Guatamalan government, Colonel Carlos Castillo Armas.

MILITARY RULE

Colonel Castillo Armas reversed most reforms that had taken place since 1944. Redistributed land was given back to the original owners, including the United Fruit Company. Trade unions were outlawed.

Castillo Armas ruled by dictatorship with the backing of the United States. Guatemalans who opposed him were tortured and imprisoned. Tens of thousands of people died from Castillo

Armas's cruel policies. Within a short time, Castillo Armas made many enemies and had several rivals for power. In summer 1957 a palace guard from an opposing group killed the president.

This cycle continued for decades. Military leaders ruled with an iron hand. Constitutional rights were abolished. Some leaders suspended elections to stay in power. One president after another was overthrown. War-weary Guatemalans grew tired of political violence.

During the 1960s rebels opposed to the military formed guerrilla organizations around the country. At first, most guerrillas were ladinos who had advanced as professionals and soldiers. Later, poorer ladinos, students, and dissatisfied soldiers joined the fight. These rebels risked their lives against the army in exchange for a fairer society. They wanted to defeat military governments in power and reinstate earlier reform programs.

The military responses against guerrillas were overwhelming. Large armies swept through cities in the countryside where guerrillas hid. Wealthy landowners hired armed men to locate government opponents and kill them. These death squads killed many peasants, students, workers, and church representatives. Often, victims knew nothing about the guerrilla groups. By the 1970s the rebel movement seemed crushed.

Throughout the 1960s and 1970s the United States supported the Guatemalan military. United States businesses invested large amounts of money in the country to build factories and develop land. Consequently, the Guatemalan economy improved. Manufacturing expanded and demand for varied crops increased. Guatemalans produced spices, flowers, and manufactured goods for export.

Cities swelled with poor people looking for factory jobs,

especially after an earthquake in 1976 destroyed many homes. Squatters in larger metropolitan areas like Guatemala City and El Mezquital built neighborhoods of shacks on the edge of town. A main Guatemala City garbage dump that was once on the outskirts of the city became the city's center because so many shacks pushed the city limits outward.

REBEL MOVEMENTS

Military violence continued unchecked. By the late 1970s surviving rebel fighters led a new round of protests. This time the guerrillas organized protesters from the cities and the western Highlands where Indians lived. Christian groups not connected with wealthy landowners joined the protests.

Government reaction was as swift as before. Sometimes large public protests in cities and towns led to sweeping massacres. The military increased violence against many Indian communities, fearing they were connected with the rebels.

Many peaceful demonstrations ended in violence against protesters. On January 31, 1980, a group called the Campesino Unity Committee (CUC) occupied the Spanish Embassy. They protested military activities in the Highlands. The Guatemalan military burned thirty-nine protesters alive in the embassy.

Military violence against rebels increased under General Efraín Ríos Montt, who became president after a military takeover in 1982. Ríos Montt introduced policies forcing villagers to serve as local soldiers. As such, the villagers had to fight against their neighbors who might be guerrillas. If they fought, the guerrillas would kill them. If they refused, they or their families would be killed by the army.

In 1984 Guatemalan refugees, masked to prevent being recognized, help themselves to dinner served by a church in Philadelphia, Pennsylvania.

This violence cost Guatemala many lives. Human rights groups estimated that more than 150,000 Indians and ladinos were murdered or kidnapped, and hundreds of villages and homes were destroyed. *Le Monde*, a French newspaper, claimed that the military committed 15 killings for every one committed by the rebels.

To escape, many Indians fled into the mountains. Some joined guerrilla groups to fight the government. Others established secret villages but kept away from the fighting. To survive, they planted crops in areas sheltered from army helicopters overhead. Since that time, generations of children have grown up in hiding.

Many more Guatemalans reluctantly left the country. Thousands of immigrants have fled to Mexico, Canada, and the United States. About fifty thousand Guatemalans are in Chicago, Illinois, alone. Several thousand more migrate with the harvesting seasons to pick crops in rural Florida.

However, the United States refuses to allow most of these refugees to stay. In response about three hundred churches and synagogues have provided safe shelter for these Guatemalans. The United States Department of Justice arrested some church activists

These Guatemalan children and their parents traveled in an "underground railroad" from Guatemala to Vermont to start a new life.

for hiding illegal immigrants. Nevertheless, church activists and human rights groups have joined together to monitor peace efforts and help Guatemalans improve conditions in their villages and in foreign countries.

Guerrilla wars in the 1980s came at a time of economic crisis. Export prices for such staples as coffee declined. Oil exploration produced little yield. Like other poor countries, Guatemala experienced a growing debt to foreign nations. To make matters worse, the United States reduced its support in response to the severe human rights violations against innocent people.

Outside pressures led to calls for elections that included several political parties and a new constitution. In 1986 voters elected President Marcos Vinicio Cerezo Arévalo from the Christian Democratic party.

Hopes were high for real change. But Cerezo faced massive poverty, a small wealthy class that paid little taxes, foreign control of the economy, and a smoldering guerrilla war. Above all, Cerezo knew a powerful army waited to overthrow him if he acted too much against their interests.

President Cerezo realized the only way to bring peace to all of

Vinicio Cerezo (left) was president from 1985 to 1991.
In 1991 Jorge Serrano was elected president.

Central America was to meet with representatives of rebel groups
However, these meetings ended without agreement. Guerrillas
wanted changes that would open politics to poor people, increase
Indian and ladino access to land, improve wages and health care,
and end military control of Guatemala. Cerezo could not agree to
these demands. He was limited by the military and the
landowners who had put him into office.

Cerezo's presidency barely had a chance. After a four-year term,
Jorge Serrano, a conservative businessman and leader of the
Movement of Solidarity Action party, was elected president. In
1993 Serrano tried to suspend the constitution and rule by
presidential powers. Security forces surrounded government
homes and news media were censored. When international and
other Latin American governments as well as local business and
political leaders criticized Serrano, he was forced to resign. Within
two weeks the National Congress elected the government's human
rights ombudsman, Ramiro de León Carpio, as president.

President De León pledged to do away with special government
accounts in millions of dollars and asked foreign governments to
increase aid. Members of the National Congress were asked to
resign, and Congressional elections are scheduled for late 1994.

Chapter 6

ONE LAND:
TWO CULTURES

Guatamala is the third-largest country in Central America. Yet its population of over ten million people is the largest in the region. The problem is not in numbers, however. It is with the great diversity and the seeming disrespect for customs of different communities. The challenge is to move Guatemala forward as one nation without destroying the value and charm of its varied customs.

LANGUAGE

Language is one of the most critical barriers to acceptance in Guatemala. Spanish is the official language. It is the language of the descendants of Spanish explorers and of the ladinos. It has become the language of power. Government affairs, business, and schooling are carried out in Spanish.

Conquerors probably viewed Spanish as a way to unite the population. Instead, the language has caused greater divisions among Guatemalans. The Indians regard Spanish as a foreign language. Although some speak Spanish, most prefer the language of their community.

A deeper problem lies in the fact that there are twenty-two indigenous communities, each with its own languages. The main languages are Quiché, Cakchiquel, Mam, and Kekchi. All others are variations of these languages. Often, members of one village cannot communicate with someone from another village. Language has been an effective barrier against communities uniting, particularly to have their say in government.

EDUCATION

The ministry of education runs Guatemala's four-level public school system. The entire system includes two years of preschool, six years of primary school, six years of secondary education, and university education. By law, only children between the ages of seven and fourteen are required to attend school.

In reality, fewer than 65 percent of primary-age children receive formal education. Educators estimate that 52 percent of the population over fifteen years of age cannot read or write. That figure soars to 80 percent in many rural areas.

The reasons for poor school attendance vary. Many families cannot afford the cost of books and uniforms. Some need their children working with them full-time. Plantation owners are required by law to maintain schools for the workers' children. However, these schools are limited in number and quality. Isolated villages are without access to nearby schools.

Even if there were schools, many view formal education as the government's way of eliminating Maya culture. Indians are

A rural schoolhouse

offended by rules that require students to wear uniforms instead
of their native dress and by history lessons that stress Spanish
conquerors and omit great Maya heroes and events.

Those rural children who do attend school go for four hours a
day from January through October. Classes are large, sometimes
as many as sixty children, and the school buildings are often
shabby and unsafe. Children bring their own lunch to school.

City schools are somewhat better. In wealthy neighborhoods,
children learn French and English in addition to the regular
curriculum of reading, writing, mathematics, and science. Still,
dropout rates are high. Only 15 percent of all students who
complete primary school continue to the secondary school level.

Secondary schools have a dual focus. The first three years cover
a general curriculum. The next three years lead to specific college
preparation or to job training, for example, for teachers, clerical
workers, and agricultural technicians.

A father and son (left) selling vegetables in Antigua, and a Maya woman (above) carrying clothes and woven belts to market in a traditional manner

There are five universities in Guatemala. The University of San Carlos, begun in 1676, is the largest. Even at this level dropouts are common and many students and faculty have been killed for their political activity.

The government has established various programs, some with the United States, to improve education in Guatemala. Peace Corps volunteers and religious groups go into communities to teach children and train adults in more modern agricultural techniques.

HEALTH

Guatemala is a nation of young people. About 46 percent of the people are under age fifteen. Disease, malnutrition, and poor health care account for a large number of deaths at early ages. Warfare continues to claim a significant number of lives. Plantation workers die from chemicals sprayed on crops, often

Children in the market (left) and townspeople attending a mobile clinic to receive prescriptions and inoculations (right)

while they are working. Infants are especially affected by harmful conditions on plantations. Forty children out of every hundred under the age of five die. Guatemalans have many children, fully expecting some will die.

It is not surprising that huge differences exist between health care in the city and rural areas. Compared to the countryside, an unusually high number of doctors, dentists, nurses, and other health care workers serve Guatemala City. Consequently, city dwellers live longer—about fifteen years longer—and healthier lives than country folk.

During the 1980s the government built six hundred rural health centers. Efforts were concentrated on training local residents in health care to relieve the shortage of doctors. Indians often prefer their own folk medicines. But the government still works to expand medical opportunities in rural areas.

Natural folk remedies have been passed down from generation to generation. Village leaders prescribe cures that use a host of

A Spanish-style building in Antigua (left); a village on Lake Atitlán (right)

leaves and herbs. They recommend evergreens and other leafy plants for pregnant women, colds, and headaches. Some call for bath water to soothe the body. Others provide much needed vitamins to give field workers energy. Many Indians believe that these plants have helped their people survive.

HOMES

The few wealthy Guatemalans live in elegant homes. Some are grand Spanish-style buildings with modern conveniences. Gardens are an important part of these estates. They encircle patios that are used for recreation and barbecues. Graceful wrought-iron fences surround these haciendas.

Poor ladinos and most Indians, however, live in simple homes of one or two rooms. Everything inside and out of the house is natural. The building materials depend on the area. Walls are wood or heavy stone blocks covered with plaster. Palm leaves or clay tiles cover the outer frame. The bare ground serves as a floor.

Few homes have electricity or indoor plumbing. Sometimes families connect two or three shacks to add rooms to the house.

Village stores are only open during the day. Long workdays mean people go to bed when the sun sets. So candles supply enough light. In the mountains, gasoline is poured over *ocote*, a piece of wood cut from a pine tree. When ignited, the wood burns for hours. For bathrooms, families use outhouses or other outdoor toilets. They bathe and draw water for cooking from rivers and streams.

A steam bath is housed in a small hut called a *temascal*. The hut has an outer shed made of adobe. Inside is another hut made of stone. To take a steam bath, the bather closes the door and lights a fire in one corner. This heats the stones. Then water is thrown against the stones to produce steam. Steam baths laced with evergreens are considered healthful for pregnant women.

On some plantations, hundreds of workers sleep in open shelters. Handmade mats protect them from the cold ground and a leaf-covered framework acts as a roof. The only privacy comes from knowing that neighbors from other villages probably speak a different language.

FAMILY

The importance of family and community varies for different Guatemalan groups. Among the wealthy and urban, the immediate family has the greatest importance. Households include parents and children, with servants to perform chores. Husbands head the family and make most business decisions. They leave household decisions regarding the children and servants to their wives. These men view women's work inside the

A Guatemalan farm family

home as a measure of a man's ability to provide for his family. In turn, the women and the children defer to the man's authority.

Within most Indian families, parents are the basis for an extended family that involves the entire community. Here village leaders are responsible for every child. These leaders can be men or women. The women receive special respect because, like the earth, they give life. Often, this difference means that women are sheltered. At fiestas, girls must stay close to an adult. Any mischief could disgrace the entire family and the community.

In poorer families, men and women have their own jobs. But Indian men and women are more likely than wealthy ladinos to share in making family decisions. Some of this equality stems from the rebel movement and greater acceptance of women as political leaders.

Every Guatemalan couple wants children. A couple that is able to have children is valued. Childless marriages are grounds for

Weaving cloth on a backstrap loom

important gods—Jesus Christ of the Catholic church and the local Maya god.

Antigua is known for the most spectacular Holy Week celebration. Among the floats are actors reenacting Christ's last hours, complete with Roman soldiers. The procession walks on a beautiful carpeted road made of sawdust and flower petals. The covering is sculpted into detailed multicolor designs. Sometimes the carpet extends for four city blocks.

ART AND MUSIC

Religion and community provide the basis for Guatemalan arts. Of all the arts, weaving best expresses these two features of Maya society. Weaving is a special language of design and color. A Maya author once wrote, "Weaving has preserved the design of the Maya universe."

Handwoven and embroidered clothing and blankets display symbols of nature and tell about individual Maya villages. Cotton or woolen threads are dyed with colors from plants and insects, much as they were during ancient times. Most women still weave on the same simple loom, called a backstrap loom, used by the early Maya.

*Carved ceremonial masks, as well as the fabrics of Guatemala,
display unique designs based on the world of nature.*

The Maya decorate pottery, wooden masks, leather engravings,
sculpture, and jewelry with the same unique designs from nature
as are woven into colorful cloth. Once completed, the crafts are
used for ceremonies or sold at the market. More modern artistic
styles can be seen in jade and silver jewelry sold in cities.

Nowhere is the harmony of village life more obvious than in
Guatemalan music. The national instrument is the marimba.
Marimbas are so large they need more than one player. It is this
team effort that symbolizes Maya communities.

Marimba rhythms accompany Maya and Christian ceremonies
from birth until death, including birthdays, baptisms, weddings,
fiestas, and funerals. Each village has its own marimba rhythm, or
son, to accompany local dances.

Marimbas are like large xylophones, with wooden bars cut to
different lengths to produce the notes of the scale. Guatemalans
build marimbas by hand out of hormingo wood. Each bar has a
resonator under it, sometimes made from a hollow gourd. The

A marimba band

resonators are tuned to their bars. The intestines of pigs are attached to the resonators to help intensify the sound. Players use small sticks with raw rubber tips to strike the bars and produce the sound.

Other handmade instruments accent lively marimba beats. Some musicians play shakers made of hollowed-out gourds and coconuts with dry beans or beads inside. Others perform with drums made from skins and wood. Guatemalan teenagers living in foreign countries preserve their folk heritage while raising money for their families in Guatemala by performing in marimba bands.

FOODS

All types of international foods are found in the cities. The dishes blend Spanish and other European influences. They feature fish and poultry with corn, beans, squash, tomatoes, hot chilies, rice,

Tortillas are cooked over a wood fire (left). Corn, tomatoes, beans, and peppers (right) are staples of the Guatemalan diet.

coconut, bananas, and other tropical fruits. Black Caribs on the Caribbean coast favor spicier *enchiladas* and *tapados* with sweet coconut breads.

Maize and beans are the basis of country foods, and many Indians prepare them as they did before the Spanish arrived. To make dough for round, flat *tortillas*, women grind the maize on an ancient stone passed down from ancestors. In some villages, women go each morning to a central corn grinder, or *molino*, to crush the corn. After water is added, the mixture turns into a pasty dough. Portions of the dough are patted into round patties to be baked on a clay plate over a fire.

Every part of the maize plant has a function. Maize can be toasted and ground for boiling in hot water. The result is a drink similar to coffee. Corncobs are cooked with lime and ground up as dog food. Some Indians say the lime keeps their dogs strong. Plant leaves are woven into mats for sleeping.

Tortillas and beans are eaten several times a day. Depending upon the area, other fruits and vegetables complete the country diet.

RECREATION

Guatemalan children enjoy many of the same activities as children of other countries. Sports are especially popular. Both boys and girls play soccer, the number one sport in Guatemala. Soccer fields are part of most school grounds. Because of the mild climate and plentiful natural resources, many Guatemalans also play basketball and baseball, go hiking and fishing, and enjoy a variety of water sports.

Playtime is limited for poor children. By the time they are eight years old, many are working beside their parents on plantations or small family farms. After everyday chores, they carve wooden objects or paint designs on bark or leather to be sold as crafts.

Still, children and their families find some time to enjoy each other. Fiestas provide the main form of entertainment. Entire communities share food, prepare special drinks from maize, and dance into the night. After work, children listen to their parents' stories about their ancestors.

Boys and girls play simple games. Boys play with shells, stones, and marbles, pitching them at a mark. Girls especially like to play their own version of house. They pick flowers and leaves and pretend to make soup. Sometimes their parents buy inexpensive dolls at the market for the girls to carry on their backs as their mothers do. The girls make miniature clay dishes to prepare foods and their mothers give them pieces of dough so they can make tortillas for their doll babies.

Everybody plays a form of freeze tag and hide-and-seek. Hide-and-seek is especially challenging in the woods or jungle.

Tourists like to come to luxurious resorts to enjoy the pleasant weather in Guatemala, but civil patrols (inset) during times of political unrest often frighten them away.

Chapter 7

A TRAVEL
THROUGH TIME

With magnificent natural resources, Maya treasures, and exciting traditional crafts, Guatemalans tried to bolster their economy with tourist trade. Private investors built hotels and constructed roads during the 1970s. By 1979, tourism became the second major cash industry after coffee. Then unpredictable political unrest during the 1980s frightened visitors. Within five years, tourism hit its lowest point.

The 1990s brought some promise of safety. Yet confidence and visitors are slow to return. Political violence continued to shatter the country. The army stations checkpoint at will on highways and side roads, particularly in the Highlands and eastern jungles.

Some tourists try to get past the disorder of Guatemala City and provincial capitals and brave the uneasy politics of the countryside. These people find magic in the primitive life-style that has remained unchanged for centuries.

ANCIENT GUATEMALA

Over the years, archaeologists have uncovered a treasure chest of complex structures that revealed secrets of the ancient Maya culture. To preserve these treasures, Guatemala joined four other

Tikal
National Park

Guatemala City

There are thousands of structures at Tikal, now a national park in Petén. The Temple of the Masks (above) and the Giant Jaguar (right) are two of the buildings thought to have been built between the sixth and the tenth centuries A.D.

nations that shared its Maya heritage to establish *La Ruta Maya*, "The Maya Route."

La Ruta Maya united Guatemala, Belize, Mexico, Honduras, and El Salvador in a project that connects 1,500 miles (2,414 kilometers) of ancient cities, remote villages, endangered tropical rain forest, and the longest rocky ridge in the Americas. One tourist visa allows visitors to reach historic destinations easily. The goal of this project is to provide access to remote Maya sites, while minimizing road building, uncontrolled settlement, and forest destruction. The overall plan complements similar government goals to conserve Guatemalan natural resources.

In 1989 the presidents of Mexico and Guatemala signed an agreement making Guatemala's northern tropical rain forests part of the Calakmul Biosphere Reserve. The agreement is an important step toward preserving Guatemala's cultural and environmental wealth. Both countries agree to keep border communities the way they were when the ancient Maya occupied the region.

Reminders of Maya brilliance abound in Guatemala. Archaeologists agree that Guatemala was the cultural center of the New World and of Maya civilization. One of the most spectacular sites uncovered is the ancient religious center of Tikal, now a national park in Petén. Over the years, archaeologists reconstructed 50 square miles (130 square kilometers) of city, with more than three thousand buildings, a huge ceremonial temple of the Giant Jaguar, and looming pyramids. Temple IV is the highest Maya structure, at 229 feet (70 meters). The jungle setting is striking, with exotic birds, spider monkeys, and other wildlife. In 1979 the United Nations Educational, Scientific, and Cultural Organization (UNESCO) declared Tikal National Park a "World

The Great Plaza was the center of Maya life in the city of Tikal.

Cultural and Natural Monument" because of its natural and Maya splendor.

Other major excavations are at El Mirador, possibly the first great Maya city; Uaxactún, with the oldest known inscribed stone slab and the first observatory; Rio Azul; and Dos Pilas. At Dos Pilas archaeologists unearthed many stelae and large stone columns. A giant stone stairway with carvings tells of warfare and other events in the city's history. Historians estimate that the Dos Pilas dynasty eventually controlled more than 2,000 square miles (5,180 square kilometers) of rain forest, perhaps the largest Maya kingdom.

CITY ORGANIZATION

Within each Guatemalan province is a capital city. Provincial capitals can be almost as large as Guatemala City, or small towns

There are many modern buildings in Guatemala City because it has been damaged many times by earthquakes. The cathedral (above right) was damaged in 1976 and is being reconstructed.

of a few thousand residents. Each town has a central market and Catholic church overlooking the main square. Most towns have similar layouts. Each is planned on a grid. *Avenidas*, or avenues, run north and south. *Calles*, or streets, run east to west. Two larger cities, Guatemala City and Antigua, are the only exceptions. But even there, the system still works in the older central parts of the cities.

GUATEMALA CITY

Guatemala City contrasts sharply with Guatemala's ancient beginnings. Unlike the peaceful, sparsely populated countryside, Guatemala City is a busy, modern city. As the country's capital and commercial center, the city is home to more than 15 percent of Guatemala's population. Guatemala City is the largest city in Central America and is still growing.

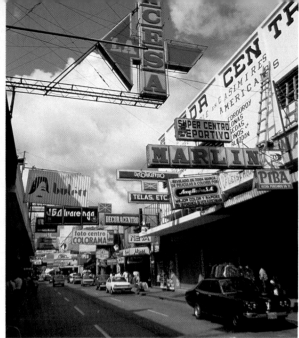

*The National Theater (left) has been constructed on the remains
of the old San Juan Fortress, which defended the old city.
A busy commercial area (right) in Guatemala City*

Guatemala City is located almost 5,000 feet (1,524 meters) above
sea level in a valley of the Sierra Madre mountains. The capital
originated in 1776 after a violent earthquake destroyed Antigua,
Guatemala's previous capital. At first, Spanish colonial buildings
dominated the city. Then the earthquakes of 1917 and 1976
demolished a great deal of the architecture. Rebuilding and urban
development altered much of the city's colonial character.

Guatemala City, more than any other, represents the most vivid
example of extremes in Guatemala. For one segment of the city's
population, modern Guatemala City has high-rise office buildings,
theaters, luxury hotels, shopping centers, universities (including
the University of San Carlos), and many museums that pay tribute
to the country's ancient heritage. So many television satellites dot
the rooftops in the southern suburbs that the metal disk is
jokingly called, "the national dish of Guatemala." Several
neighborhoods near the heart of the city and in suburbs house
wealthier residents.

Left: Modern buildings have ancient Maya designs.
Right: Slums of Guatemala City

Many other city residents, however, live in poverty. For them, the city grew faster than its ability to accommodate everyone who came seeking jobs and a better life. These people live in shacks in crowded ravines that were once the city dump. Unable to find work, they scavenge the dump for food and things to sell. Orphaned children beg or sell whatever they can in the streets. The children cannot afford books or uniforms for school. Many turn to cheap drugs, such as inhaling rubber cement fumes, thinking they can escape their problems.

Armed guards are everywhere—on tree-lined suburban streets or in front of fast-food restaurants. Carrying guns and being stopped for weapons checks have become a fact of life everywhere in Guatemala. And nowhere is it more obvious than in the city. Although Guatemala City has lively discos and theater, few people venture out after dark.

Volcán Agua overlooks the city of Antigua (left).
The University of San Carlos de Borromeo (right)

Guatemala City

Antigua

ANTIGUA

Twenty-five miles (forty kilometers) west of Guatemala City is
Antigua, officially called Antigua Guatemala. Antigua's location
in a valley surrounded by three large volcanoes—Agua, Fuego,
and Acatenange—adds to the town's exceptional beauty. The
grand Agua volcano to the south is visible from anywhere in
town, and the Fuego always smokes.

Antigua is a well-preserved colonial city that was the nation's
second capital, from 1543 to 1773. The Spanish conqueror, Pedro
de Alvarado, chose the town as the seat of Spain's "new
kingdom" for its central location. He urged the Catholic church to
spend large amounts of money to make Antigua the grandest city
in Latin America.

Monks from several orders came to convert and teach the
Indians. The Convent of the Capuchins became the center of study
and meditation for nuns who followed. The University of San
Carlos opened here in 1681. At its peak, fifty-five thousand people
lived in Antigua.

To try to protect the buildings in Antigua from earthquakes, the walls were thickly built and reinforced. Church ruins (left) and buildings near Santa Catarina Arch (right) are evidence that this did not always work.

Much of the old city was shattered by two major earthquakes— in 1773 and 1976—and many smaller earthquakes, fires, and floods. Yet the city still retains its beauty and is a favorite among visitors.

Today, about twenty-seven thousand people live in Antigua. Ruins of cathedrals, convents, plazas, officers' residences, and government buildings remain as reminders of Spanish rule. The university is a museum of colonial art. The many churches hold elaborate pageants to celebrate Guatemala's religious past and present, especially during Holy Week. Recently, an ancient Maya quarry near Nejar reopened. Now Antigua is a noted center for buying quality jade.

Because of the city's renowned museums and fine examples of Spanish colonial art, the Pan American Institute of History and Geography declared Antigua a "Monument of the Americas" in 1942. Later the United Nations named the city "Heritage of Humanity."

Quezaltenango

QUEZALTENANGO

Quezaltenango is Guatemala's second-largest city, with about 300,000 people. It is located in the western highland mountains 7,800 feet (2,377 meters) above sea level. People of Quezaltenango have Quiché Maya origins. The city was originally the site of the Quiché Maya ancient capital of Xelaju. Spaniards later named the town Quezaltenango. But Indians and some bus signs still refer to the city as Xelaju, or Xela.

Quezaltenango was the first Spanish settlement. The city still has the oldest colonial buildings in the country. Old suburban Quezaltenango follows the same urban design as Antigua. Classical architecture with grand columns, such as those adorning the Municipal Theater, blend with traditional costumes of Indians selling goods at the market. As with other highland towns, the

The semicircular front steps of the Church of San Tomás

surrounding mountain scenery is breathtaking. Nearby are volcanoes, thermal springs, mountains, rivers, and valleys where coffee, wheat, fruits, and vegetables grow and cattle are bred.

CHICHICASTENANGO

Chichicastenango is a small town of about sixty-five hundred people in the central Highlands. Many Guatemalans view this village as a combination of their two great cultures. Ancient rituals and Catholic ceremonies are performed side-by-side regularly. Services at the Church of San Tomás, which dates back to the mid-1500s, honor local patron saints in addition to universal Christian traditions. Hillside caves that can be seen from the town square are still used by the Indians for the same ceremonies as those that took place during earlier times.

The primary purpose of the market in Chichicastenango is
to sell goods such as fabric and clothes (above) or wood (below),
but it is also a time to meet friends and gossip.

Centuries ago, Chichicastenango was the location where the *Popol Vuh* was discovered. This ancient Maya "Bible" was the first of several books on stone uncovered in overgrown ruins.

Normally, Chichicastenango is a peaceful town with narrow cobblestone streets. But every Thursday and Sunday the town comes alive with colorful markets. Local Indians in traditional dress offer handmade weavings, wood carvings, and ceramics in open stalls. Afterward, buyers watch sellers participate in religious ceremonies.

LIVINGSTON

The Caribbean town of Livingston is unlike any other in Guatemala. The reason is the large number of blacks, who make the town seem like a West African village. These blacks are descendants of Carib Indians and African slaves.

They live rather isolated lives and have their own traditions. Women wear head scarves and unadorned costumes. Throughout Livingston, residents play their version of music with strong African drumbeats and speak an *Arawak* (Caribbean Indian) language as well as Spanish. Nearby is the Chocon Machacas Biotope, a preserve for manatees and mangroves.

AN INDEPENDENT NATION

Travelers to Guatemala can experience many wonderful sights of today and long ago. There are great Maya civilizations of the past, grand examples of Spanish influence, and evidence of the successes and failures of an independent Guatemalan nation.

Government administration buildings in Guatemala City

Chapter 8

GUATEMALA TODAY

Guatemala's hope of curbing poverty lies in its ability to organize a fairer government and economy. As the people speak out for democracy, they may reach the goal.

GOVERNMENT

According to the May 1985 constitution, Guatemala is a republic with three branches of government: executive, legislative, and judicial. By law a president is the chief executive who governs the nation for a single five-year term. Presidents and their vice-presidents are elected officials, who must receive 51 percent of the votes. Similar to other Western countries, Guatemala's president chooses a cabinet of ministers to help manage government operations.

A National Congress represents the legislative branch of government. Its elected members serve one or more five-year terms. The one-hundred-member Congress drafts Guatemalan law.

Laws are enforced through the judicial branch. The judiciary handles cases on a local level in Peace Courts. There also are a Court of Appeals and a Supreme Court, Guatemala's highest court. The president appoints judges to the Supreme Court. In turn, high court representatives select the judges for lower courts.

Guatemala includes twenty-two administrative departments, or provinces. Each department has an elected governor. Departments are further divided into municipalities governed by elected mayors and councils. Local governments carry out national government policy rather than creating their own programs.

Although the Indians outnumber ladinos in many regions, few become government officials. In the countryside, Indian villagers choose their own leader and committee of elders. These leaders are responsible for community activities and decisions. Indian leaders are chosen early in life. Boys and girls are selected as village spokespersons as soon as they demonstrate outstanding thinking, artistic, and social skills.

The real power behind the Guatemalan government lies with the army and wealthy landowners and industrialists. Military officers ignore the constitution to overthrow presidents who devise policies they dislike. They kidnap, kill, and torture civilians to keep their favored government in control. To date, these human rights abuses continue largely unhampered by Guatemala's frightful judicial system.

ECONOMY

Historically, the government has left the economy to private sources. The result has been slow growth and uneven distribution of wealth, with the rich getting richer and the poor getting poorer. A 1988 study found 8 percent of Guatemala City laborers were out of work, 17 percent worked only part-time, and 12 percent were grossly underpaid.

Family farms are often very small patches of tilled soil.

More recently the government has tried to expand economic development and vary its foreign trade partnerships. Government social programs have opened some jobs to service and office workers. Still, a majority of the population works as poorly paid farm laborers, craft workers, or small farmers.

AGRICULTURE

Guatemala's economy is based on agriculture. Farming employs about 60 percent of the work force and supplies 67 percent of the country's exports. Yet the very basis of the economy is also its weakness. Farming reinforces the great divisions between small family farmers and large commercial operations that supply crops for export.

Most farmers plant tiny family patches, some the size of cemetery plots. About 90 percent of the farmers own small farms.

Tending new coffee plants

But they hold only 16 percent of the farmland. On this land, poor Guatemalans cultivate mainly corn, beans, and squash, keep sheep for wool, and raise chickens and pigs. The farmers use simple tools, such as *machetes*, long knives, to chop weeds and hoes to till the ground. Any extra food is sold at the market. To make ends meet, entire families leave their homes to work on large plantations. Some go to the city to find limited factory or domestic jobs.

A handful of ladinos own the country's most fertile land. Large plantations account for 65 percent of the land, while amounting to only 3 percent of the total number of farms. Many of these large farms utilize powered plows and pesticides that sometimes cause sickness or death from chemical poisoning among field-workers. When crops like coffee require gentle handling, overseers hire busloads of cheap labor from the Highlands. In some areas Guatemalans pick crops all day for very meager wages.

Coffee is the country's main crop, making up more than one-third of Guatemala's export income. Between growing and

Sorting coffee berries

processing, coffee employs 25 percent of the population. Other major crops for export include sugar, bananas, macadamia nuts, and cardamom, a spice. More recently, cattle production increased enough to permit Guatemala a sizable amount of meat for export. Unfortunately, the extra meat is shipped out of the country at a time when more than 50 percent of the children under five years of age have been starving.

Fishing contributes about 1 percent to the nation's agricultural economy. Most inland fishing is for local sale. Nevertheless, commercial fishing is a growing industry. Major fishing operations are along the Pacific coast. Here waters teem with mackerel, salmon, shrimp, and tuna.

FORESTRY

Guatemala has large tracts of valuable forested areas. However, extensive logging for commerical purposes, farming, and energy has reduced the number of trees and caused severe erosion.

Researchers claim that 90 percent of all timber cut during the 1980s was for cooking, coffee roasters, and pottery kilns. Recent government limits on logging have changed the focus of the logging industry. Now the goal is to encourage greater investment for extracting products from trees such as chicle (the base for chewing gum), vanilla, sarsaparilla, camphor, cinnamon, and barks and herbs used in medicines.

INDUSTRY

Factory output increased during the last quarter of the twentieth century but at a slow pace. Manufacturing tends to be concentrated in Guatemala City, where there are few jobs compared to the large numbers of unemployed people. Here and in the countryside people have little money to buy anything but basic necessities. Therefore, little demand exists for manufactured goods within Guatemala.

Manufacturing accounts for only 16 percent of the economy. Factories concentrate on processing foods, beverages, tobacco, textiles, rubber, paper, leather, and medicines. Guatemala has one of the oldest candy companies in Latin America. It produces more than one hundred kinds of candies that are flavored and designed to look like fresh fruits.

An important growth area involves assembly plants, where raw materials are sent for processing. The government has created several tax incentives to attract foreign investors who want to take advantage of Guatemala's cheap labor. Legislators also devised tax-free zones throughout the country to encourage development of industry in locations other than Guatemala City.

Tax-free zones provided a small amount of industrial expansion

Guatemalan pottery

and some additional jobs, but this growth did little for most Guatemalans. Without taxes, the government lacked money for much-needed social programs to improve health and housing.

The backbone of Guatemalan industry remains the individual and small business owner. Indians specialize in craft production of textiles, pottery, baskets, wood carvings, and painted tiles. Other small businesses in villages include bakeries, gas stations, and repair shops—anything that relies on hand labor.

PRODUCTION OF NATURAL RESOURCES

The national economy profits from large deposits of minerals and oil. Major investment in oil exploration occurred during the 1970s. Foreign companies built refineries in the Alta Verapaz Province, with a 100-mile (161-kilometer) pipeline to the east coast port of Santo Tomás de Castilla. Although only a small refinery at Escuintla exists today, the government is seeking outside investors to extract large amounts of untapped oil in reserves in the Petén region. Today, many investors fear that political fighting will interfere with oil exploration.

The government looks to hydroelectricity from the country's many waterfalls to reduce dependence on imported oil. The production of electricity has increased, mainly through construction of two large power plants at Chixoy and Aguacapa. Future plans include expansion and export of electric power to neighboring countries.

Mining contributes a relatively small portion to the economy. Large nickel deposits lie north of Lago de Izabal. At one time North Americans and Canadians contributed to the Exmibal project that produced vast quantities of nickel. The mine has shut down, due to the collapse of nickel sales, but it can be revived when world prices of nickel rise. A jade quarry reopened near Nejar to provide high-quality jadeite. Jade is sold as gemstones or carved into sculpture or jewelry. Guatemala also holds sizable deposits of copper, antimony, and tungsten.

TRADING PARTNERS

Guatemala's main trading partner remains the United States. In 1961, Guatemala joined its neighbors in the Central American Common Market (CACM) to establish additional markets for goods. The CACM, responsible for considerable growth in manufacturing for the next ten years, has declined. Guatemala has entered into trade agreements with Honduras and El Salvador, to ease entry into NAFTA, the North Atlantic Free Trade Agreement.

Jade will be processed from these rocks (top left). Buses (bottom left) are used for transportation between cities that are connected by highways (above).

TRAVEL

Guatemalan travelers fly on Aviateca, the government-owned airline. Aviateca supplies most domestic and international services. The only international airport is in Guatemala City. Chartered small aircraft fly tourists to remote ancient ruins. A little-used national railway system makes more than fifty stops along 500 miles (805 kilometers) of track. The fifteen-hour trip is painfully slow.

Two Atlantic coast ports, Santo Tomás de Castilla and Puerto Barrios, are managed by the state port authority. Santo Tomás serves shipping lines from the United States, Europe, and Central and South America. The Pacific coast maintains the newer Puerto Quetzal, which is connected to Guatemala City and Atlantic ports by highway and railroad.

An extensive network of paved highways connects major cities and towns around the country. Several bus companies operate between towns of any size and the capital. Minibuses serve

103

This man (left) carries a heavy load of water jugs in a traditional manner, as do these women carrying baskets on their heads (above).

smaller communities, stopping at city centers where merchants have shops.

Once travelers are in town, taxis are available for transport. Few Guatemalans own cars, especially in the country. Many roads through the Highlands are impassable by anything other than foot travel. Heavy loads are still carried over backs or on top of heads as in earlier Maya times. People in the country are used to walking up to six miles (ten kilometers) to shop.

COMMUNICATION

Guatemala has five television channels and about seventy radio stations. The government runs one radio and one television station. Everything else is privately owned. Wealthy city viewers watch Cable News Network (CNN) and HBO broadcast from the United States, in addition to soap operas from Mexico. Although repeating towers broadcast signals throughout Guatemala, most of the poorer population is without television or radio.

Guatemala has four major privately run newspapers that supply information throughout the country. The major cities receive regular shipments of several international newspapers, some in foreign languages.

The arts have become one avenue for telling Guatemala's story to the world. Enrique Gómez Carrillo was a noted author who lived between 1873 and 1927. Miguel Angel Asturias earned the 1967 Nobel prize in literature for his series of stirring novels about Guatemala, including *El Presidente, Strong Wind,* and *Mulatto Woman.* Otto Rene Castillo, a poet, wrote about revolutionary struggles during the 1960s and the life of poor people.

Dramatic studies of Guatemalan life have been prepared outside the country by supporters of human rights causes. *I, Rigoberta Menchú* is a moving book translated from interviews with Rigoberta Menchú, a Quiché freedom fighter who was awarded the Nobel Peace Prize in 1992. *El Norte* was the first English film documenting the dangerous route villagers take from rural Guatemalan villages to the United States and the problems migrant Guatemalans face in a new country.

GUATEMALA'S FUTURE

With all its natural beauty and economic potential, Guatemala is still a troubled place. Centuries of hostility between descendants of Spanish-Americans and the Maya show few signs of easing. Sporadic clashes between the army and rebels have made travel, and often living, dangerous. In spite of these problems, Guatemala is a magical country. For all its people, it is a land worth fighting for—fighting for peace.

MAP KEY

Antigua Guatemala	C2	Morales	C3
Asunción Mita	C3	Motagua (river)	C3
Ayutla	C1	Moyuta	C2
Barillas	C2	Ocós	C1
Chahal	C3	Panzós	C3
Champerico	C2	Pasión (river)	B2
Chimaltenango	C2	Patzicia	C2
Chinajá	B2	Patzún	C2
Chiquimula	C3	Piedras Negras	B2
Chiquimulilla	C2	Polochio (river)	C3
Coatepeque	C2	Pto. Barrios (point)	C3
Cobán	C2	Quezaltanengo	C2
Comalapa	C2	Retalhueleu	C2
Concepción	C2	Sa de Los (mountains)	B2, C2
Cuchumatanes (mountains)	C2	Salamá	C2
Cuilapa	C2	Salinas (river)	C2
Cuilco	C2	Samalá (river)	C2
Dolores	B3	San José	D2
Escuintla	C2	San Luis	B3
Flores	B3	San Luis	C3
Gualán	C3	San Marcos	C2
Guatemala (Gautemala City)	C2	San Pedro (river)	B2
Guazacapan	C2	Sanarate	C2
Huehuetenango	C2	Santa Cruz del Quiché	C2
Huixtla	C1	Sarstún (river)	C3
Jalapa	C3	Sierra Madre (mountains)	C1, C2
Jutiapa	C3	Tapachula	C1
L. de Izabal (lake)	C3	Tikal (ruin)	B3
La Libertad	B2	Tiquisate	C2
Livingston	C3	Totonioapán	C2
Los Amates	C3	Usumacinta (river)	B2
Mazatenango	C2	Volcán Tajumulco (volcano)	C1
Momostenango	C2	Zacapa	C3

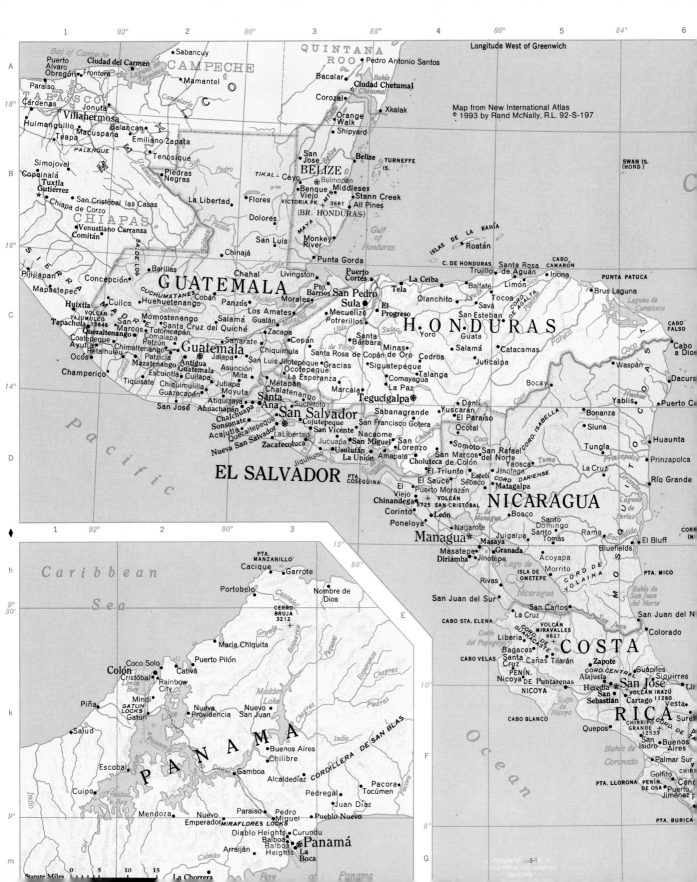

Pigs for sale in the market at San Francisco

The charming courtyard of a small inn in Antigua

About the Authors

Marlene Targ Brill is a free-lance Chicago-area writer, specializing in fiction and nonfiction books, articles, media, and other educational materials for children and adults. Among her credits are *John Adams* and *I Can Be a Lawyer* for Childrens Press; *Washington, D.C. Travel Guide*, a regular column for the secondary publication, *Career World*; and contributions to World Book Encyclopedia's *The President's World* and *Encyclopaedia Britannica*.

Ms. Brill holds a B.A. in special education from the University of Illinois and an M.A. in early childhood education from Roosevelt University. She currently writes for business, health care, and young people's publications and is active in Chicago Women in Publishing and Independent Writers of Chicago.

Ms. Brill has written *Libya, Mongolia,* and *Algeria* in the Enchantment of the World series. She would like to thank her husband, Richard, and her brother, Harry Targ—her two geography and history consultants.

Harry B. Targ is a professor of political science and American studies at Purdue University in West Lafayette, Indiana. He has written and edited books and articles on United States foreign policy, United States political economy, Nicaragua, and Cuba. Mr. Targ's book *People's Nicaragua* was published in 1989; another book, *Cuba and the USA: A New World Order?*, was published in 1992. *Plant Closings: International Context and Social Costs*, written with Carolyn Perrucci, Robert Perrucci, and Dena B. Targ, was published in 1988.

Professor Targ received a M.A. in political science from the University of Illinois and a Ph.D. in political science from Northwestern University.

Professor Targ affirms his love for Dena Targ, Rebacca Targ, and Genevieve Targ. Marlene Targ Brill, his sister, is not so bad either.